Breaking Generational Curses

Breaking Generational CURSES

By Mimi Lowe

XULON PRESS ELITE

Xulon Press Elite
2301 Lucien Way #415
Maitland, FL 32751
407.339.4217
www.xulonpress.com

Scripture quotations taken from the New King James Version
(NKJV). Copyright © 1982 by Thomas Nelson, Inc. Used by
permission. All rights reserved.

Edited by Xulon Press.
Printed in the United States of America.

ISBN-13: 9781545643181

Contents

Preface

*D*o you sometimes struggle with inexplicable thoughts or actions? Are there unusual patterns in your family such as rampant divorces, early deaths, suicides, alcoholism, or drug abuse? Do you ever feel like you are stuck? Are there times when you feel something is wrong, but you cannot seem to put your finger on it? Perhaps the answer lies within these pages.

The purpose of this booklet is to inform readers about the reality of curses on our lives and our families that are the consequences of sins committed by our ancestors in our generational lines. I do not claim that all problems are rooted in generational curses, but suggest that they could be contributing factors.

Within these pages, I share testimonies of people who have experienced freedom through prayers of repentance and forgiveness. I also highlight a selection of the scores of Scriptures related to this often controversial topic in order to confirm its scriptural validity. While not intending to downplay the importance of Scripture, my hope is that the testimonies will speak for themselves.

I have also included sample prayers with each testimony. If you feel that any of these prayers apply to your situation, please feel free to use them and modify them to fit your own circumstances if necessary. It is my desire that you walk in the freedom Jesus procured for each of us at the Cross.

1

What is a Generational Curse?

A generational curse is the consequence of the sin or sins committed by our ancestors, often referred to in the Bible as the "sins of the fathers." (Exodus 20:5, Exodus 34:7, Numbers 14:18, Deuteronomy 5:9). In other words, when our ancestors sinned, the consequences of that sin put in place curses that affected all of their succeeding generations and each of their descendants.

What is sin?

Sin is transgression and rebellion against God and His laws.

Whoever commits sin also commits lawlessness, and sin is lawlessness. (1 John 3:4)

1

> The heart is deceitful above all things,
> And desperately wicked;
> Who can know it?
>
> I, the Lord, search the heart,
> I test the mind,
> Even to give every man according to his ways,
> According to the fruit of his doings. (Jeremiah 17:9-10)

When we sin, we reap the consequences of our sin if we do not repent or seek God's forgiveness and make any necessary restitution. Even if no one knows or sees what we have done, our sin and its consequences will affect us as well as our descendants. The spiritual law of sowing and reaping is universal and timeless. We reap what our ancestors sowed, just as our children will reap what we have sown.

If our thoughts, actions, words, or deeds are honorable, then blessings will flow into our lives and will also be reaped by our succeeding generations. On the contrary, if our thoughts, actions, words, or deeds are sinful, and we do not repent of our sins, we will suffer the consequences of our sinful actions, and so will our descendants.

> Do not be deceived, God is not mocked; for whatever a man sows, that he will also reap. For he who sows to his flesh will of the flesh reap corruption, but he who sows to the Spirit will of the Spirit reap everlasting life. And let us not grow weary while

doing good, for in due season we shall reap if we do not lose heart. (Galatians 6:7-9)

Even as I have seen, those who plow iniquity
And sow trouble reap the same. (Job 4:8)

2

If You Have Bad Fruit, There is a Bad Root Somewhere

Have you ever noticed negative patterns in your family? For example, a son has a problem with uncontrolled anger, his father has the same problem, and his grandfather also struggled with anger. Or, out of the blue you suffer from fear for no reason, or depression comes upon you without warning, and you discover that your mother or father had the same issues.

Why is this?

The sins of our forefathers, or generational sins, always carry consequences. This does not mean that God is punishing us for the sins committed by our ancestors. As God's children, we have been forgiven because of Jesus' death on the cross and His victorious resurrection. We are no longer held accountable for their sins.

However, the enemy of our soul, Satan, is a legalist. When our ancestors sinned, they opened a door to the enemy, allowing him access and permission to wreak havoc in their lives and the lives of future generations. The enemy has the right to continue the harassment until we acknowledge the sin and repent. If repentance does not occur during the life of the one who committed the sin, the consequences are passed down to the descendants.

The good news is that we also inherit generational blessings, according to the same principle of sowing and reaping, as a result of the righteousness of our ancestors. Think about yourself for a moment. What have you inherited from your mother? Your father? Your grandparents on your mother's side? Your grandparents on your father's side? A few answers might be physical features, personality and character traits, likes and dislikes, strengths and weaknesses, mannerisms, godly characteristics, or musical and artistic talents and skills. Even genuine faith can be passed down generationally, as we read in the Bible.

> (The Apostle Paul speaking to Timothy) ...when I call to remembrance the genuine faith that is in you, which dwelt first in your grandmother Lois and your mother Eunice, and I am persuaded is in you also. (2 Timothy 1:5)

Should we have had perfect and sinless ancestors, which is highly unlikely, since Scripture says that we all fall short of the glory of God (Romans 3:23), we would still have trials, tribulations, challenges, and obstacles to overcome.

> These things I have spoken to you, that in Me you may have peace. In the world you will have tribulation; but be of good cheer, I have overcome the world. (John 16:33)

Our children will inherit some of our memories, along with some of our parents' and grandparents' memories. We tend to inherit our ancestors' positive and negative mindsets and attitudes, which are reflected in our choices, our preferences, and in the way we think and act.

Just as we can trace the negative attitudes and behaviors back to our parents, grandparents, and previous generations, we can also trace the positive attitudes and behaviors back through our ancestral line as well. Has anyone ever said to you that your personality traits or characteristics reminded them of your great grand mother, or your great grand father, or grand mother, or grand father, or aunt or uncle or some other person that they knew who was related to you?

As an exercise, take a personal and family history of issues in your life, much like your physician would take your medical history. This will enable you to observe patterns of issues throughout your generational line that are affecting you or your extended family. At the same time, look for the generational blessings that are in your family line and how these blessings are evident in your life and in your family's lives.

Look at the list in Deuteronomy 28 and see what curses or issues may be in your life. Here is a partial list of some common patterns:

- Alcoholism, drug addictions, or other addictions, such as gambling, shopping, or eating
- Inexplicable illnesses or premature deaths
- Multiple miscarriages, barrenness, infertility, abortions
- Consistent financial losses, business failures, or lost inheritances
- Occult involvement
- Sexual sins or pornography
- Emotional problems, such as depression, anger, fear, rejection, or abandonment
- Family relationship difficulties, such as feuds, divorces, or unresolved conflicts
- Patterns of tragedies or accidents
- A sense of something preventing you from going forward, like hitting an unseen wall

- Unusual or abnormal thought patterns or mindsets that cannot be shaken off

Just as curses come down the generational line, blessings also pass down the generational line, such as:

- Having families, parents, children, and loved ones all knowing the Lord Jesus Christ
- Family unity and peace
- The absence of early deaths, divorces, miscarriages, accidents, financial losses, addictions
- The work of your hands is blessed (Deuteronomy 28:12)

Deuteronomy 7:9

> "Therefore know that the Lord your God, He is God, the faithful God who keeps covenant and mercy for a thousand generations with those who love Him and keep His commandments;

3

What is the Biblical Basis for Generational Curses?

Numerous scriptures state that sin, especially idolatry, leads to generational curses that have a direct effect on our descendants to the third and fourth generation. If the following generation sins, then the generational curse continues on further down the generational line.

> You shall not make for yourself a carved image - any likeness of anything that is in heaven above, or that is in the earth beneath, or that is in the water under the earth; you shall not bow down to them nor serve them. For I, the Lord your God, am a jealous God, visiting the iniquity of the fathers upon the children to the third and fourth generations of those who hate Me, but showing mercy

to thousands, to those who love Me and keep My commandments. (Exodus 20:4-6)

And the Lord passed before him and proclaimed, "The Lord, the Lord God, merciful and gracious, longsuffering, and abounding in goodness and truth, keeping mercy for thousands, forgiving iniquity and transgression and sin, by no means clearing the guilty, visiting the iniquity of the fathers upon the children and the children's children to the third and the fourth generation." (Exodus 34:6-7)

'The Lord is longsuffering and abundant in mercy, forgiving iniquity and transgression; but He by no means clears the guilty, visiting the iniquity of the fathers on the children to the third and fourth generation.' (Numbers 14:18)

'... you shall not bow down to them nor serve them. For I, the Lord your God, am a jealous God, visiting the iniquity of the fathers upon the children to the third and fourth generations of those who hate Me ...' (Deuteronomy 5:9)

It is imperative that we worship the one and only true Creator God, who alone is King of kings and Lord of lords (Revelation 17:14, 19:16, 1Timothy 6:15). Worshipping of idols or foreign gods opens the door to the enemy to bring curses and destruction into our lives. Because of God's love and mercy, God's blessings come down the generational line to a thousand generations if our ancestors loved God and were faithful to Him. In God's economy, the blessings of God far outweigh any curses.

Through the atoning work of His death and resurrection, our Lord Jesus Christ legally dealt with every curse and every legal requirement of the law.

> Christ has redeemed us from the curse of the law, having become a curse for us (for it is written, "Cursed is everyone who hangs on a tree) (Galatians 3:13)

> Therefore, if anyone is in Christ, he is a new creation; old things have passed away; behold, all things have become new. (2 Corinthians 5:17)

Our sins have been forgiven, and we are a new creation in Christ redeemed, forgiven, and reconciled to our Father in Heaven. However, our adversary, the enemy of our soul, is a legalist and will cause us to reap the consequences of our ancestors' sins until we repent of their sin which is part of working out our salvation.

> Therefore, my beloved, as you have always obeyed, not as in my presence only, but now much more in my absence, work out your own salvation with fear and trembling. (Philippians 2:12)

Even though the Apostle Paul was redeemed from the law and his sins forgiven, he was still not perfected.

> Not that I have already attained, or am already perfected; but I press on, that I may lay hold of that for which Christ Jesus has also laid hold of me.

> (Philippians 3:12)

4

Biblical Principles for Breaking Generational Curses

*U*sing the principles of repentance laid down by the Old Testament prophets Nehemiah, Jeremiah, Daniel, many people have been freed from the chains that kept them captive as they repented on behalf of their ancestors for the sins that were committed generations ago. This is sometimes referred to as identificational repentance. We identify with the sins of our ancestors and repent on their behalf, and God in His grace and mercy accepts our prayers of repentance on their behalf and remembers it no more. The majority of people, when asked what they sensed after the process of generational repentance prayer, said they felt lighter, as if a heavy load had been lifted off. This freedom clears the way for generational blessings to be released.

Nehemiah and his associates prayed the following prayers in the context of the return of the Jewish people from the Babylonian exile and the great restorative task of rebuilding the wall of Jerusalem.

> "Please let Your ear be attentive and Your eyes open, that You may hear the prayer of Your servant which I pray before You now, day and night, for the children of Israel Your servants, and confess the sins of the children of Israel which we have sinned against You. Both my father's house and I have sinned. We have acted very corruptly against You, and have not kept the commandments, the statutes, nor the ordinances which You commanded Your servant Moses." (Nehemiah 1:6-7)

"Now therefore, our God,
The great, the mighty, and awesome God,
Who keeps covenant and mercy:
Do not let all the trouble seem small before You
That has come upon us,
Our kings and our princes,
Our priests and our prophets,
Our fathers and on all Your people,
From the days of the kings of Assyria until this day.

However You are just in all that has befallen us;
For You have dealt faithfully,
But we have done wickedly.

Neither our kings nor our princes,
Our priests nor our fathers,
Have kept Your law,
Nor heeded Your commandments and Your testimonies,
With which You testified against them.

For they have not served You in their kingdom,
Or in the many good things that You gave them,
Or in the large and rich land which You set before them;
Nor did they turn from their wicked works." (Nehemiah 9:32-35)

Jeremiah prayed the following prayer when he beseeched the people of Israel to repent of their generational sins in order to avert the impending Babylonian invasion and exile of Israel from the promised land.

For shame has devoured
The labor of our fathers from our youth -
Their flocks and their herds,
Their sons and their daughters.

We lie down in our shame,
And our reproach covers us.
For we have sinned against the Lord our God,
We and our fathers,
From our youth even to this day,
And have not obeyed the voice of the Lord our God. (Jeremiah 3:24-25)

Daniel prayed the prayer of generational repentance below when he understood that the seventy years of Babylonian exile prophesied by Jeremiah were completed and the time had come for the exiles to be restored to Jerusalem.

Then I set my face toward the Lord God to make request by prayer and supplications, with fasting, sackcloth, and ashes. And I prayed to the Lord my God, and made confession, and said, "O Lord, great and awesome God, who keeps His covenant and mercy with those who love Him, and with those who keep His commandments, we have sinned and committed iniquity, we have done wickedly and rebelled, even by departing from Your precepts and Your judgments. Neither have we heeded Your servants the prophets, who spoke in Your name to our kings and our princes, to our fathers and all the people of the land. O Lord, righteousness belongs to You, but to us shame of face, as it is this day - to the men of Judah, to the inhabitants of Jerusalem and all Israel, those near and those far off in all the countries to which You have driven them, because of the unfaithfulness which they have committed against You. "O Lord, to us belongs shame of face, to our kings, our princes, and our fathers, because we have sinned against You. To the Lord our God belong mercy and forgiveness, though we have rebelled against Him. We have not obeyed the voice of the Lord our God, to walk in His laws, which He set before us by His servants the prophets." (Daniel 9:3-10)

"O Lord, according to all Your righteousness, I pray, let Your anger and Your fury be turned away from Your city Jerusalem, Your holy mountain; because for our sins, and for the iniquities of our fathers, Jerusalem and Your people are a reproach to all those around us." (Daniel 9:16)

5

Testimonies

$\mathscr{F}$ollowing are accounts of people who are believers in the Lord Jesus Christ, yet were struggling with various issues. Since receiving prayer for generational sin and generational strongholds, their lives have been changed. The fruit of these testimonies is undeniable. For the sake of confidentiality, the names used in this material are pseudonyms. Results include, but are not limited to, people coming to Christ, drawing closer to the Lord Jesus Christ, reconciling with family members and friends, and breaking down walls of hostility.

I have included an example of the prayer that was prayed after each testimony. If you feel you are experiencing the same or similar issues, you can use the prayers as a starting point and adapt them to your specific circumstances.

Curses Related to External Circumstances

Generational Fraud - Sarah's Testimony

For many years, Sarah had difficulties with insurance companies, whether in relation to her home, her car, or her personal insurance. At times, she could not get insurance. At other times, her insurance policy lapsed, and she was not informed about it, but only became aware when she needed to make a claim. I asked if anyone in her generational line had problems in this area. Sarah shared that her grandfather purposely burnt down his business to collect on the insurance policy. His crime was never uncovered. I led Sarah in a prayer to repent on behalf of her grandfather for arson, defrauding the insurance company, cheating, dishonesty, deceit, illegal gain, and destruction of property. After her prayers of repentance on behalf of her grandfather, Sarah had no further problems with insurance companies.

Here is a sample prayer if you feel you have experienced the same or similar issues as Sarah:

In Jesus' name, I repent on behalf of all my ancestors, especially on behalf of my grandfather, (insert whoever committed the crime) for arson, fraudulent claims against insurance companies, cheating, dishonesty, deception, illegal gain, conspiracy, fraud, and destruction of their own property, stealing, robbery, and lies. Lord Jesus, please release me from the consequences of the sins of my ancestors, especially from the consequences of the sins of (name the person), in Your Name, I pray. Amen.

Bullying

On several occasions, I have prayed for men and women who were bullied as children and, in most cases, their children were also bullied. Sometimes their ancestors were bullied, or they were the bullies. I would lead the person to pray prayers of repentance for generational bullying, intimidation, maligning of character, criticism, vilification, ruining a person's reputation, and anything else along those same lines. Following this, the person would pray a prayer of forgiveness to those who were the victimizers. Usually, the person experienced freedom from bullying almost instantly.

This is Al's testimony:

From my childhood to my adult working life, I can remember being a victim of bullying. It was not physical intimidation, but rather mental and emotional. At work, I would often end up working for or with bullies who would mistreat me professionally, and I could never win. We got revelation from the Lord that a lot of my grief came as a result of my mother's father. He was a bully who fought in bars and intimidated most people around him. I later heard that his father had not accepted him. It then became obvious that this pattern had been going on for many generations. I went through the healing process of forgiveness and repentance. My situation at work improved gradually, and the bullies became much less prevalent, and eventually the bullying stopped completely.

Here is a sample prayer you may wish to pray if you struggle with bullying, harassment, or intimidation:

> ### The Cause of many instances of bullying is often rooted in our Generational Line.

In the name of Jesus, I repent and renounce on behalf of my ancestors from the beginning of time to the present and especially on behalf of (here name the person if you are aware of such a person) for bullying, for verbal abuse, intimidation, and cruelty, especially against those who are vulnerable, weak, or disenfranchised. I repent on behalf of all my ancestors and especially on behalf of (here name the person if you are aware of such a person) for maligning, defaming, and slandering people. I repent on behalf of all my ancestors and especially on behalf of (here name the person if you are aware of such a person) for harassment and stalking, for demeaning people, defamation of character, and for mocking and cursing people. I repent for all generational acts of dishonor, disrespect, and devaluing of personhood. I repent for all generational spewing out of discouraging words and words that debilitate and paralyze. I repent on behalf of all my ancestors and especially on behalf of (here name the person if you are aware of such a person) for crushing peoples' spirits and destroying their futures. I repent on behalf of all my ancestors for belittling, insulting, humiliating, shaming, and destroying peoples' reputations. Lord, I extend forgiveness to all those who have bullied me, maligned me, and caused me pain. Lord, I bless those who have hurt me, and I bless them with salvation, in Jesus' name. Amen.

Oppression

Those whose ancestors were slaves can sometimes suffer from poverty, lack, failure, oppression, and the inability to rise up to take their rightful place in their home, their workplace, or society. The person must forgive slave traders or slave owners for taking their ancestors away forcefully from their land, for dividing up families, for putting a price tag on them, for inhumane treatment, for torture, for causing untimely death, for victimization, for injustice, for robbery of dignity, for robbery of freedom, for oppression, for never paying them what they were entitled to, and other indignities. These are a few examples of the long list of atrocities committed in relation to the slave trade.

A declaration should then be made to release the person to grow and blossom as God intended and ordained. It is also beneficial to validate and legitimize them as human beings. They may need to be released from generational limitations, since their ancestors were restricted in every facet of their lives, so that they are no longer victims but conquerors in Christ Jesus.

Here is a sample prayer if you struggle with oppression or similar issues:

In Jesus' name, on behalf of myself and my ancestors, I extend forgiveness to the slave owners and slave traders for removing my ancestors from their native land and for forcefully separating them from their loved ones. On behalf of myself and my ancestors, I extend forgiveness to those who put a price tag on my ancestors, subjected them to public humiliation, shame, oppression, and inhumane treatment. I extend forgiveness to those who tortured my ancestors, caused untimely deaths, and victimized them. Lord Jesus, on behalf of myself and my ancestors, I extend forgiveness to the victimizers for robbery of dignity, robbery of freedom, robbery of dreams and visions, withholding and denying my ancestors their wages, for injustices, and for robbing them of their identities. Lord, I extend forgiveness on behalf of myself and my ancestors to the perpetrators for crushing their spirits and for causing them to become hopeless and helpless. Lord Jesus, please release me and my children (or child) from the consequences of the sins of the slave owners and slave traders and release me and my children (or child) from the spirit of victimization so that we are no longer shackled and chained, and we are no longer limited, but free in Jesus' name to be all that God has ordained us to be. In Jesus' name, we can do all things through Christ who strengthens us. Amen.

Boundaries or Limitations - Carl's Testimony

A gentleman of American Aboriginal descent named Carl felt that whenever he moved outside of his birthplace, ill fortune came upon him. I led him to pray on behalf of himself and his ancestors to forgive the "white men" for placing ungodly boundaries and limitations on his ancestors. We prayed that God would disconnect him from the ungodly boundaries set by the "white man," and that he would be free to travel wherever he felt led to go. We also prayed that God would release him from the ungodly limitations that affected his life. He experienced freedom immediately and is now able to travel freely.

Here is a sample prayer if you feel you struggle with the same or similar issues:

In Jesus' name, on behalf of my ancestors and myself, I forgive all those who placed ungodly boundaries and ungodly limitations on my ancestors. On behalf of my ancestors and myself, I extend forgiveness to those who robbed us of our freedom and our dignity as human beings.

Lord Jesus, please release me and disconnect me from the ungodly boundaries set by those who victimized us so that I may be free to travel wherever the Lord would lead me. Lord Jesus, in Your name, please release me from all ungodly limitations that came down the generational line. Amen.

Career or Permanent Employment - Joan, Bob, and Erin's Testimonies

I have encountered many people who have experienced problems with keeping a job. They would work for a week, a few months, or a year, and then they would lose their jobs for various reasons. This would repeat time after time, job after job. I have found that in this area, there is no single solution to the problem. Each person has their own generational history of employment, and often the issues can be complex based on the historical background.

Here are some employment-related generational issues that I have encountered:

Joan's father owned his own business and routinely fired people for unfounded reasons. The consequence of this injustice affected Joan as she experienced job loss on a regular basis. Since repenting on behalf of her father for unjust dismissal of his employees, Joan has been able to maintain stable employment.

Here is a sample prayer if you feel you share the same or a similar struggle as Joan:

In Jesus' name, I repent on behalf of my father (or ancestor) for firing people from his (or her) business for unjust causes. I repent on behalf of my father (or ancestor) for anger, selfishness and greed. I repent on behalf of my father (or ancestor) for being an unjust and unfair employer and disregarding the welfare of his (or her) employees. Lord, please release me from the consequences of my father's (or ancestor's) sins, in Jesus' name. Amen.

Bob's ancestors were Aboriginal and were prohibited from doing a "white man's job." He could not get a job until this blockage was removed through prayers of repentance and forgiveness.

Here is a sample prayer if you feel you share the same or a similar struggle as Bob:

In Jesus' name, I forgive all those who forbid my ancestors from doing "a white man's job." I forgive those who oppressed and suppressed my ancestors. Lord Jesus, please release me and my descendants from declarations and proclamations that were put in place to prohibit my ancestors and myself and my descendants from exercising their rights as individuals, in Jesus' name. Amen.

Erin's ancestors were of Irish descent. Years of severe famine in Ireland in the mid eighteen hundreds brought many starving and destitute men, women, and children to America. They came threadbare, poor, and sickly. The Irish were Catholics and there was an anti-Catholic, anti-Irish and anti-immigrant sentiment in America during that period of time, especially in the area of employment. The new immigrants were seen as a threat to the job security of Americans. The sign "NINA" appeared in many shop windows, which meant "No Irish Need Apply." The Irish were also deeply hated because of their Catholic faith. As a result of praying prayers of generational repentance and forgiveness, Erin was able to obtain employment and no longer suffered the consequences of her ancestors' circumstances.

Here is a sample prayer if you feel you share the same struggle as Erin:

In Jesus' name, I extend forgiveness to all those in past generations who refused to hire people of Irish (or other ethnicity) descent. I extend forgiveness to all those who murdered, killed, and plundered our homes and our lands because of our heritage. I extend forgiveness for the hatred and rejection of the Irish (or other ethnicity) and denying us the right to earn a living.

In Jesus' name, please release me from the generational curse against the Irish Catholics (or other ethnic or religious group). Please release me from the unfair and unjust stigma that came down the generational line, in Jesus' name. Amen.

Financial Loss

Financial loss is another complex issue, since there are so many individual historical reasons for losses in this area. Loss of a home, continuous financial loss in business or investments, or losing one's inheritance are just a few examples of the effects of financial curses. People who struggle to make ends meet or experience continual thievery are candidates for this category as well. When finances are constantly being drained, a person might feel like they have holes in their pockets. Generationally speaking, issues such as thievery, robbery, dishonest gain, not tithing (giving God His portion), not taking care of widows and orphans, idolatry, and disobedience to God can all play a role in the area of chronic financial problems.

Here is an example of a prayer that could be prayed against financial curses:

In Jesus' name, I repent on behalf of myself and my ancestors, going back to the beginning when financial loss, poverty, and robbery were empowered. In Jesus' name, I repent for generational idolatry, pagan worship, witchcraft and sorcery, for rebellion against God and for disobedience to the commandments and precepts of God. Lord, I repent for generational dishonesty, thievery, robbery, dishonest gain, dishonest scales, and cheating. In Jesus' name, I repent on behalf of all my ancestors for not helping widows and orphans, for exploiting and stealing from widows and orphans, and for not helping those in need.

In Jesus' name, I repent on behalf of all my ancestors for greed, for the withholding of resources from those in need, for stealing of inheritances, and for the withholding of tithes and offerings. In Jesus' name, I repent on behalf of all my ancestors for cheating the government, for cheating on income taxes, and for fraud. Lord, please release me from the spirit of financial loss and poverty, in Jesus' name. Amen.

This is a generic prayer that can be prayed, but we need to examine our generational line, with the help of Jesus, to find out what happened to bring about specific losses in the area of finance. We can then pray repentance on behalf of the person or people in our family line who committed the sins and forgive those who did financial harm to our ancestors, so that consistent financial loss and failure will end. A longer, more extensive, prayer for financial release can be found at the end of this booklet. Also, see Deuteronomy 8:18-20.

Sexual Immorality in Children

Generational curses can impact children as well as adults, including curses of fear, anxiety, anger, or sexual sin. I have prayed for children who have had unusual sexual behaviors. The youngest child I prayed for was three years old. In this particular case, I looked at the history of this child's parents and grandparents and found sexual immorality and the same ungodly sexual behaviors that were exhibited by the child. In instances in which the children are very young,

I do not have the children in the same room as the parents. It is not necessary for them to hear their parents pray about ancestral sexual sins. It is sufficient for the parents to pray prayers of repentance for their own sins and on behalf of their ancestors.

Here is an example of the prayers I have led parents to pray:

In Jesus' name, I repent on behalf of (insert 'myself' if necessary) and all my ancestors, going back to the beginning of when these sins first took root, for rape, incest, adultery, fornication, lust, sexual sin, sexual perversion, bestiality, sodomy, pornography - for defiling the body, defiling the eyes, and defiling the spirit. In Jesus' name, I repent on behalf of (insert 'myself' if necessary) and all my ancestors for masturbation and prostitution. Lord, please release my child/children from the consequences of my sins and the sins of my ancestors, in Jesus' name. Amen.

Testimony of a Child Set Free from Challenging Behavioral Issues
Below is an email I received from Esther, who adopted little Angela. Angela's biological parents were both addicted to drugs, and her biological mother continued to ingest drugs while pregnant with her. Consequently, Angela was born with a drug addiction and had to go through a withdrawal process. She had extremely challenging behavioral issues from birth.

Thanks so much for coming out last week. Wanted to give you a brief update. Angela is completely different! She's so much calmer. Maybe twice a day she becomes angry, as opposed to at least twice an hour. When she does become angry, it's a typical five-year-old's response. Previously, the anger was overwhelmingly demonic. Our new foster child arrived the day after you came. He's in his own world with limited words and comprehension. Angela used to get frustrated with the older foster girls here because she easily understood things they did not. So far with the new boy, she's been incredibly patient and nurturing (characteristics not previously displayed). When he cries for no apparent reason, Angela tries to comfort him. In the past when another child would cry, she'd yell at them to shut up.

She still gets annoyed with Johnny (the neighbor's boy who was here when you came), but not to the previous degree, and she's able to spend long stretches of time interacting with him positively.

On Monday when Jane (the babysitter who was here when you came) watched Angela and Billy, the new foster child, Angela complained of being bored. She just sat and read while the kids played. Angela used to need adult intervention about every ten minutes. Even her thirst for attention is diminished. Jane, who interacts with Angela on a regular basis, is completely amazed at the transformation.

Angela is finally at peace. In her own words, 'I feel good. Before Mimi prayed, I felt bad.' As I write this, she's actually sharing her special toys!

Thanks so much! This has been so beneficial. I was growing very weary dealing with Angela, but now, with so much cleared up, it's a much easier journey. Thank you!

Blocked Communion - Jane's Testimony

Jane was puzzled as to why she could not receive communion at church. She was able to attend church, but there seemed to be an unseen force blocking her from receiving communion. No matter how hard she tried to receive the sacraments, she could not get past this spiritual wall that prevented her from partaking of the Holy sacraments. She repented on behalf of her ancestors for blasphemy of the communion elements, for receiving communion when their hearts were not right with the Lord, for mocking and ridiculing the elements, and for the desecration of the elements. The following Sunday, the blockage left, and Jane was able to receive communion.

Here is a sample prayer if you feel you share the same struggle as Jane:

In Jesus' name, I repent on behalf of all my ancestors for blaspheming the communion elements, for mocking and ridiculing the communion elements, for desecrating the communion elements, and for taking communion when their hearts were not right with the Lord. In Jesus' name, please release me from the consequence of my ancestors' sins. Amen.

Family Estrangement

When there is hatred between family members, with no apparent cause, it is possible that there may have been a murder committed between similar family members in the ancestral lineage.

On a mission trip to India, a Christian man shared with me that he was estranged from his brother. They had no animosity towards each other, but it seemed that whenever they were together, they could not communicate or connect. They would depart in frustration and disappointment. The Lord impressed upon me that there was a generational murder between two brothers in their ancestral line. Once this man repented for this and extended forgiveness, he and his brother were able to enjoy each other's company, as they had always desired. Consequently, his brother and their father, who were not believers at that time, became Christians.

A similar situation involved a father and his adult son. The son had rejected his father and refused to have anything to do with him. The father was puzzled because he could not think of anything that he had done that would have offended his son. I suggested that perhaps there was a murder committed between a father and a son in their generational line. Once the father repented for this and extended forgiveness, the son no longer rejected him.

Friends of mine, Phil and Sandy, had been married for about forty years. They argued and verbally fought with each other almost daily throughout their married life. They had gone through a gambit of pastors, counsellors, and therapists. Finally, in desperation, Sandy cried out to God, "What is wrong here? What is the root of our problems?"

Sandy sensed that the Lord revealed to her that there had been a murder of a child between her ancestors and Phil's ancestors. The murder was committed either by Phil's ancestors or by Sandy's ancestors. The Lord did not give any other specifics regarding this incident. They spent much time repenting on behalf of both of their ancestral lines for the murder of the child and extended forgiveness. The transformation between Phil and Sandy was indescribable. Sandy shared how her negative thought patterns about her husband changed. Not only were they transformed, but their adult children's lives and attitudes changed for the better as well.

Family/Tribal Murder and Feuding

Many times, in our ancestors' lineage, there is hatred, murder, betrayal, robbery, or injustice between siblings, between husbands and wives, between parents and children, between family members, or between separate families. Other times, people of a particular tribe or family line were at odds with those of a different tribe or family line, similar to the Romeo and Juliet story or the feud between the Hatfields and the McCoys. In generations past, Catholics and Protestants were forbidden to intermarry, and in many cases were not allowed to speak to each other. As a result, much innocent blood was shed, not only between the Catholics and the Protestants, but also between opposing tribes and warring families.

Here is an example of a prayer you can pray if any of these situations resonate with you: (Please adjust the prayer to fit your circumstances.)

In Jesus' name, I repent on behalf of all my ancestors and my husband's/wife's/brother's/sister's ancestors for murders they committed and feuds they perpetuated. In Jesus' name, I repent for all jealousy, envy, betrayal, treason, unforgiveness, resentment, bitterness, and anger between my ancestors and (here you can name some people in relationship with you)'s ancestors. In Jesus' name, I repent for all war between our ancestors, for the shedding of innocent blood, and for all hatred between our ancestors because of opposing religious or political beliefs. In Jesus' name, please break the power of any ungodly agreements, vows, or oaths that my ancestors and (name of people in relationship with you)'s ancestors made with regard to never forgiving one another and never allowing their children or any of their descendants to become friends or marry one another. Lord, in Jesus' name, please remove all walls of division and separation between us and release us in the spirit of reconciliation and unity. Amen.

Familial Hatred

Another ungodly pattern I have come across is generational hatred of a son or daughter. If the firstborn is hated and rejected in the ancestral line, then the pattern of hatred and rejection of the firstborn is perpetuated into the subsequent generation. The same applies if the second or third born child is hated or rejected in the generational line. As a result, the second or third born children among their descendants inherit the same hatred and rejection, and so on. This same principle can also be applied to generational favoritism, jealousy, injustice, abandonment or any other issue that may be evident and can at times be traced back to the family's lineage.

Here is an example of a prayer that can be prayed if this situation resonates with you, making the necessary changes to suit your circumstances.

In Jesus' name, I repent on behalf of myself and all my ancestors back to the beginning of when favoritism or hatred or rejection or injustices first took place. I repent on behalf of myself and all my ancestors for showing favoritism or hatred or rejection or injustices towards their children while rejecting the firstborn (or insert whichever child is appropriate). I repent on behalf of myself and all my ancestors for sacrificing the firstborn (or insert whichever is appropriate), for killing of the firstborn (or insert whichever is appropriate), for abortions, and for not valuing the gift of children that comes from God. I repent on behalf of myself and all my ancestors for verbal, physical, and sexual abuse of the firstborn child (or insert whichever is appropriate) in my family line. I repent for generational abandonment of the firstborn child (or insert whichever is appropriate) and for denying the existence of the child. In Jesus' name, please release me from the consequences of these sins in my generational line. Amen.

Miscommunication and Misinterpretation - Zara's Testimony

Zara wrote this testimony:

I grew up in an environment of extreme miscommunication and misinterpretation. My parents, my three siblings, and I were constantly at odds with one another. Daily strife, frustration, and anger at home also spilled over onto our relationships with friends. My words were misconstrued no matter how careful I was in expressing myself. As a married adult, the problem persisted between my husband and I. At times, it was exhausting repeatedly trying to explain myself.

We discovered the root of our problem when we found out that our grandfather was in the military during World War II. At times, he was called upon to interpret on behalf of his superiors to the townspeople in the villages because he was the only person available who could speak German. We do not have any details or know of the circumstances why the interpretation may have been incorrect. We *assume there may have been some misinterpretations or miscommu-nications to cause such strife in our family.*

After I repented on behalf of my grandfather for misinterpreta-tion and miscommunication, I experienced a significant change in my communications with my husband and with my family.

Here is a sample of the prayer Zara prayed, if you feel you are experiencing the same or similar issues.

In Jesus' name, I repent on behalf of all my ancestors, especially my grandfather (or other ancestor), for misinterpretation and miscom-munication. I repent for any negative effect, damage, or harm caused as a result of my ancestors' and my grandfather's (or other ancestor's) actions. I personally repent for miscommunication and misinterpre-tation that I may have been a part of in any way. Lord, please release me from the consequences of my sin, my ancestors' sin and my grand-father's (or other ancestor's) sin in the area of miscommunication and misinterpretation, in Jesus' name, Amen.

6

Curses Related to Internal Issues

Superstition - Steve's Testimony

One day in a café, I met a gentleman named Steve who shared with me a generational fear and superstition of being photographed that had become a problem in his everyday life. He hated being photographed, and therefore did not have any pictures of himself - not even wedding pictures. He told me his ancestors also had the same fear. I led him in a prayer of repentance on behalf of his ancestors for fear and superstition of being photographed. A picture was taken of him immediately after the prayer, and he was peaceful and no longer afraid.

Here is a sample prayer for any superstitions in your ancestral lineage:

In Jesus' name, I repent on behalf of my ancestors for superstition and for their superstitious fears and beliefs of being photographed [insert any other superstitions]. Holy Spirit, please release me from the consequences of my ancestors' superstitious beliefs and fears of being photographed. Amen.

Anger - Mary's Testimony

Mary was troubled by her unexplainable behavior. She experienced uncontrollable rage when she was faced with injustice. She knew it was out of character for her to behave in this manner. Just hearing about a situation of injustice at work, even if she was not involved, caused uncontrollable anger and rage within her. This was baffling to her as well as to her coworkers. We prayed through her generational lines about injustices, especially those against women. Eventually her rage subsided, and she was free.

Here is a sample prayer should you feel you identify with Mary's unfounded rage:

In Jesus' name, I repent on behalf of myself and on behalf of all my ancestors from the beginning where injustices and anger and rage took place; injustices, especially against women; betrayals; treasons; for causing untimely deaths; and for all murders and killings because of injustices. Lord, I repent on behalf of all my ancestors for their silence in the face of injustices. Lord, I repent on behalf of myself and on behalf of my ancestors for anger, rage, retaliation, revenge, unforgiveness, and hatred. Lord Jesus, in Your Name, please release me from the consequences of the generational sins of my ancestors especially in the areas of injustices, anger, and rage. Amen.

Unforgiveness - Ann's Testimony

No matter how hard Ann tried, she could not forgive even the smallest offense. Ann shared that her mother struggled with the same issue, and we sensed that her grandmother may have had the same challenge. Ann repented on behalf of her mother and all those in her generational line for unforgiveness and holding grudges, resentment, bitterness, and anger. We also repented for vengeance and retaliation. After her prayers of repentance on behalf of her ancestors, Ann no longer struggles in the area of unforgiveness.

Here is a sample prayer if you feel you share the same struggle as Ann:

In Jesus' name, I repent on behalf of myself and on behalf of my mother (and any other direct relative that you are aware of with the same issue) and all my ancestors where unforgiveness first took root, for refusing to forgive, for vowing never to forgive, and for holding grudges, anger, rage, resentment, bitterness, retaliation, and vengeance. Lord Jesus, I repent for generational murders, killings, rape, pillaging, stealing of inheritances, injustices and betrayals. Lord Jesus, please release me from the consequences of the sins of my ancestors, in Your Name, I pray. Amen.

Guilt, Shame, and Blame - Joe's Testimony

Joe is a strong Christian man, but he was tormented by his tendency to blame others for things for which they were clearly not guilty. At times, it was Joe's own fault, and he knew it, but he still placed the blame on others. He was guilt-ridden by his behavior, but could not change. He had repented over and over again, but could not shake this sinful habit.

Joe shared with me that as a very young boy his father was wrongly blamed for the accidental death of his baby brother. The circumstances of the baby's death were vague, but Joe's grandparents were negligent and did not want people to know, for fear of reprisal. Joe repented on behalf of his grandparents for false accusation, for placing the blame and guilt on the innocent, for forcing their son to carry a burden of guilt and shame, and for lies, deception, and negligence. Joe was instantly set free from the irrational behavior of blaming others. He also felt a heavy burden lift off his shoulders. It was the yoke of guilt and shame placed on his father by his grandparents that Joe had inherited.

Here is a sample prayer if you feel you struggle with the same or similar issues as Joe:

In Jesus' name, I repent on behalf of myself and on behalf of my grandparents (name the appropriate person or persons) for false accusations. I repent on behalf of my grandparents (name the appropriate person or persons) for negligence in the untimely death of their child. I repent that they did not take responsibility for their mistakes and placed the blame, guilt, and shame on my father, who was innocent of any wrongdoing. I repent on behalf of my grandparents (name the appropriate person or persons) for hiding the truth and for concealing their error. In Jesus' name, please release me and my descendants from the consequences of my grandparents' (name the appropriate person or persons) sins. Amen.

Anxiety around answering the Phone

Some people have anxieties associated with things as simple as answering the telephone. During times of war, going back to the early 1900's, women in particular became afraid to answer the phone, as they dreaded receiving bad news about their loved ones in the battlefield. Or, their husbands or sons would be waiting at home for the dreaded phone call sending them out to the battlefront. Waiting for the ringing of the phone often brought anxieties and fears.

41

This is just one reason people may have anxiety when they hear the phone ring. I have led people to pray prayers of repentance on behalf of their ancestors for anticipating the worst when the phone rings, and for seeing the telephone as a bearer of bad news. I have also led them in prayers to disconnect themselves from the fears, dread, and anxieties that came down the generational line in connection with the telephone or other forms of communication. They reported that after the prayers, the anxiety was replaced with peace.

Here is a sample prayer if you experience anxiety when answering the phone or similar issues:

In Jesus' name, I repent on behalf of myself and on behalf of my ancestors for our feelings of anxiety, fear, and dread whenever the phone or doorbell rang. Lord, I repent on behalf of myself and my ancestors for anticipating the worst and for seeing the telephone as a bearer of bad news. I repent that I and my ancestors did not place our trust in You, Lord Jesus.

Lord, please release me from the fears, dread, and anxieties that came down the generational line, in Jesus' name. Amen.

Fear of Flying - Charles' Testimony

Charles was healed from anxiety brought on by the fear of flying. He wrote this testimony:

For many years I had struggled with a deep fear of flying on airplanes. I would have anxiety for days before boarding and during the whole flight - constantly feeling afraid that something catastrophic would happen. I had received some prayer for fears, but the problem still persisted. I probably inherited these unfounded fears from my father, who also had anxieties and fears of flying on planes.

While Mimi was praying for me, she sensed that an ancestor had been a fighter pilot and had been forced to fly where his life would be in danger from enemy planes. He had understandably been affected by these traumatic experiences.

After we prayed for a release from the generational fears and memories, I felt free from anxiety and peaceful about the thought of flying.

A week later I had a transatlantic flight and was able to enjoy the entire flight without any fear or anxiety.

Here is a sample prayer similar to Charles' prayer that you may pray if you identify with Charles' fears.

In Jesus' name, I repent on behalf of my ancestor for the fears and anxieties he (or she) experienced because he (or she) was being deployed into enemy territories. Lord, I repent that my ancestor did not place his (or her) trust in You, In Jesus' name, on behalf of my ancestor, I extend forgiveness to those in authority for sending my ancestor into harm's way.

In Jesus' name, I ask that You would release me from the fears and anxieties that came down the generational line. Set me free, so that I may enjoy the pleasure of flying. Amen.

Fear - Joan's Testimony

Joan was plagued with feelings of fear and terror, as if there were people chasing after her. These feelings were very real to her. As we inquired of the Lord for the root of these feelings, He revealed to us that during a time of war, her ancestors were hunted down. After praying through this situation, Joan experienced a sense of peace.

Here is a sample prayer similar to Joan's prayer that you can pray if you identify with Joan's fears:

In Jesus' name, on behalf of my ancestors, I forgive those who pursued them and threatened them with death. In Jesus' name, please release me from the consequences of war, killing, and murder. Please release me from the fear and terror of being chased and hunted down. Amen.

Claustrophobic Fears - Mimi's Testimony (My own Personal Testimony)

One day, I was in an unusually heavy traffic jam. I could not move. Cars surrounded me. A claustrophobic feeling came over me, bringing with it anxiety and fear. I felt an overwhelming need to get out of the car and run. I asked the Lord for the root cause of these feelings. The Lord showed me that during a time of war, when my ancestors were trapped in a building, the enemy encircled them with the intent to kill them.

This is a sample prayer that I prayed to release myself from these feelings which you may pray if you feel you struggle with similar issues:

In the name of Jesus, I forgive the perpetrators for wanting to kill my ancestors. I forgive them for entrapment, for threats of death and for causing my ancestors to be trapped and causing them terror and fear. In Jesus' name, please release me from the feelings of being trapped and the feelings of anxieties and fears. Amen.

Fear of Loss - Lilly's Testimony

Lilly had an overwhelming fear of her house being burnt down. There weren't any logical reasons that she knew of for this fear. Fears of loss, homelessness, and being attacked accompanied this fear. We sensed that in Lilly's generational line her ancestor's house, land, and crops were deliberately destroyed by fire. Lilly was led to pray a prayer to the Lord, asking forgiveness for those who burned down her ancestors' house. She was subsequently set free from the irrational fear that was not hers to begin with.

Here is a sample prayer if you identify with the fear of loss or similar issues:

In Jesus' name, I forgive those who burned down my ancestors' home, and burned their land and crops. I extend forgiveness to those who caused my ancestors to be homeless, destitute, hopeless, and in despair. In Jesus' name, I forgive the attackers for terrorizing and attacking my ancestors. Lord, please release me from the generational fear of losing my house by fire and homelessness, the fear of destitution, and the fear of being attacked. In Jesus' name. Amen.

Suicidal Thoughts - Mimi's Testimony (My own Personal Testimony)

Suicidal thoughts come in different intensities. For some, suicidal thoughts are just thoughts that could be easily brushed off, but for others, they may be stronger urges to commit suicide. There are also those who tragically succumb to the thoughts and actually commit the act. In the vast majority of these cases, there is known suicide in the family line. In my own life, my mother did not want to live and attempted suicide on several occasions. My sister committed suicide at a young age. There were times in my life when I did not want to live but was too afraid to commit suicide. After praying through these issues, the Lord set me free from suicidal thoughts and feelings of hopelessness and despair.

Here is what I prayed which you may pray if you struggle with thoughts of suicide.

In Jesus' name, I repent on behalf of myself and my ancestors, especially my mother and sister, (or name the person or persons in your family or family line) for suicide, rejection of life, hopelessness, and despair - for not turning to You, Lord, for help in our time of need. I personally repent for embracing and partnering with the spirit of death, suicide, helplessness, hopelessness and despair. I repent for not embracing the gift of life that God gave me. In Jesus' name, I chose life. Lord, I repent on behalf of all my ancestors, and especially on behalf of my mother and sister, (or name the person or persons in your family or family line) for opening the door to the spirit of death and suicide, helplessness, hopelessness, and despair. In Jesus' name, please release me from the spirit of death and suicide, helplessness, hopelessness and despair. I close the ungodly door that my ancestors, and specifically my mother and sister, (or name the person or persons in your family or family line) opened in Jesus' name. Amen.

> *Do you sometimes struggle with inexplicable thoughts or actions?*

Murderous Thoughts - Lucy's Testimony

Lucy struggled with unusual thoughts whenever she saw or handled knives. She is a loving mother with three small children and would never dream of hurting them in any way. Yet, the sight of knives would bring about thoughts of murdering her children.

Obviously, this was a generational issue, since this mindset was so uncharacteristic of her. Lucy repented on behalf of all her ancestors for the murders of their children, even though she did not know of anyone in her generational line who had committed such an atrocity.

Here is a sample of the prayer Lucy prayed that you may pray if you feel you struggle with unusual thoughts but make the necessary changes to fit your circumstances.

In Jesus' name, I repent on behalf of all my ancestors who murdered and slaughtered their children using knives. I repent on their behalf for all abortions, the hatred of children, and the rejection of God's gift of children to them. Lord, please release me from the consequences of these atrocities committed by my ancestors, in Jesus' name. Amen.

Car Accidents and/or Fear of Driving a Car - Liza's Testimony

While in England, I met Liza. She hated driving her car, especially during inclement weather. Driving was never a pleasant experience for her, and caused her to feel anxious and fearful. She shared how her grandfather's mode of transportation was a horse-drawn wagon, and all his children got a ride in the wagon to and from school, except Liza's father, John. He was rejected as a young boy and was forced to walk a mile to and from school, no matter what the weather was. John had to endure the shame, humiliation, and rejection of never being able to enjoy the same privilege as his siblings. Understandably, John was angry with his father and his siblings. Throughout his childhood, John cursed his father and the horse-drawn wagon and wished that it would break down so that he could arrive at his destination ahead of his siblings. Consequently, Liza and her siblings have all experienced car accidents. Liza repented on behalf of her father for cursing and wishing his father and siblings harm and for cursing the horse and wagon. Once Liza repented and prayed prayers of forgiveness, she was completely free from her fear of driving from that day forward.

Here is a sample prayer if you feel you share the same or similar struggle as Liza. Please make the necessary changes to this prayer according to your own particular circumstance.

In Jesus' name, I repent on behalf of my grandfather (or other ancestor) for rejecting his (or her) son, John (or other ancestor). I repent on his (or her) behalf for shaming and humiliating his (or her) son (or other ancestor), and for showing favoritism towards his (or her) other children (or other ancestors). I repent on behalf of my father (or other ancestor) for cursing his (or her) father (or other ancestor) and his (or her) siblings and for cursing his (or her) father's (or other ancestor) horse and wagon (or other people or objects). I repent on behalf of my father (or other ancestor) for his (or her) anger, rage, bitterness, resentment, and unforgiveness toward his (or her) father (or other ancestor). In Jesus' name, please release me from the consequences of my grandfather's and my father's (or other ancestors') sins. Amen.

Emotional Healing – Jim's Testimony

I have always been aware that even though you are a Christian, you still have problems. It seems that most of us learn to live with it or give up hope. What you showed me is that there are roots to everything.

I have always read in the Bible about generational curses and spiritual oppression, but never really understood how it works. Then I met you, and you prayed for me. When you interviewed me and started praying, I realized that I, like many others, have always prayed about the symptoms, not the root causes. God showed up! I've never experienced God on such a personal level like that before. I didn't realize how much unforgiveness had kept me in so much bondage. I literally felt God break chains, lift weights, and I literally saw Jesus meet with me and show me how much He loves me.

I know that a lot of Christians will not want to believe what I say, but healing, deliverance, and visions are all biblical, and no one can take away what God has done for me. You brought me back to a painful period in my life. When I was a little boy, I thought it was hokey, until I saw myself as a little boy, and then encountered God's angels and Jesus Himself. I think everyone there had tears in their eyes. You also brought me to a place of my heritage, where my American Indian ancestors had to forgive my white ancestors for very painful things. It was so real that I didn't want to forgive at first, but then you led me through the process. My life has completely changed because of this prayer. Everyone needs this kind of prayer. I know it sounds weird to some people - it did to me at first - but no one can take away what God did for me. Thank you, Mimi!

Fear of Premature Death - Troy's Testimony

Troy sent the following testimony:

I have battled fears of premature death for years. Many times in my life, I would get a little cold, a rash, feel something weird on my body or in my body, and jump to a negative conclusion. Not only that, I would start thinking that this minor ailment would lead to my death. Fears abounded. I sought ministry, listened to teachings, and gained some measure of healing. This time around, I had a peculiar rash and a cold/cough that didn't seem to want to clear up. With a mysterious rash and this cold, I once again fell into the depths of despair and drudgery. I called Mimi, and she prayed with me. Her ministry brought increased freedom, love, and peace. As we talked, Mimi asked if anyone in my family had died prematurely. Sure enough, my grand-mother had siblings who died at an early age. All her life, she lived with the fear of death. We prayed about that and then went deeper. We asked Holy Spirit for revelation. He gave it. We saw that my ances-tors had been prematurely killed. Moreover, my Jewish ancestors were threatened with death if they didn't convert to Christianity or follow the ways of foreign leaders. The threat of death to control my ancestors' behavior was real.

Mimi led me in a prayer similar to this:

Father, on behalf of myself and my family line, all the way back to the beginning of time, I repent and renounce for all my ancestors who didn't trust you or stay faithful to you, even if it meant their lives. Forgive us, Lord, when we put our own lives ahead of worshipping You and You alone. Also, I choose to forgive, on behalf of myself and my family line, all those who threatened my ancestors with physical death or torture if they didn't obey them or bow down to their gods. I release them, Jesus, and give them to You at the Cross. Lord, I repent espe-cially for those people who persecuted Your chosen people, the nation of Israel, who controlled them and threatened them with death - or even killed them - when they didn't do what they wanted. I forgive them, Jesus, and declare them forgiven by You, Jesus, on the Cross. You paid for their sins, iniquities, and transgressions. Lord Jesus, please release me from the grip of death that takes hold of me when I am weak and vulnerable, in Your name, I pray. Amen.

We also prayed that when I get sick, I wouldn't immediately go into the depths of despair and Sheol - that I would continue to stay in health and life, in Jesus' name.

After our prayer session together, I felt lighter - like the power behind the fears of death had been broken. They no longer held the same sway they did before. Something shifted, and I was in a better place.

7

Final Thoughts

*W*as the concept of generational sin and generational curses new to you? Do you recognize any struggles in your life, or the lives of your loved ones, or friends, that may be the result of generational sin?

Regardless of your views, may I suggest that you thoughtfully consider the prayers and scriptures within this book that specifically deal with this important issue? My desire is that this book may give you revelation and understanding of the hidden roots of inexplicable situations and sometimes complex, or not so complex, challenges that arise in our everyday lives.

For those who are dealing with generational curses or strongholds in your lives, it is my prayer and desire that as you trust in God and wholeheartedly and sincerely pray prayers of repentance and forgiveness on behalf of your ancestors, you will experience glorious freedom. May you go forward and share your life-changing experience with others, giving glory to God.

8

General Release Prayers

J usually encourage people to pray the following prayer because most of us have ancestors who did not follow God and His ways. Just going back ten generations, there are over 4,000 ancestors, and the chances are extremely high that there were some who dabbled in the occult.

Generational Prayer for Occult Practices

In the name of Jesus, I repent and renounce on behalf of all my ancestors from the beginning of time to the present for witchcraft, sorcery, and shamanism.

Lord, I repent and renounce on behalf of all my ancestors for pagan worship and all worship of gods and goddesses.

Lord, I repent and renounce for all generational worship of trees, the worship of the earth, and the worship of the moon, sun, and stars.

Lord, I repent for all generational worship of the elements.

In Jesus' name, I repent and renounce on behalf of all my ancestors from the beginning of time to the present for all involvement with druidism.

Lord, I repent and renounce for any of my ancestors who were druids. I renounce their occult practices, especially human sacrifices and cannibalism.

In Jesus' name, I repent for their killings and murders by drowning, stabbing, and burning for the purposes of appeasing their gods or for gaining power and favor.

I repent for their ungodly use of their power and authority.

I repent for all generational evil rituals and evil ceremonies.

I repent for all magical potions and evil incantations.

I repent on behalf of all my ancestors for the belief in magical healing and for the drinking of magical potions and applying of magical ointments.

In Jesus' name, I repent on behalf of all my ancestors from the beginning of time to the present for all séances and mediums. I repent for conjuring up the dead and conjuring up demons, for evil dedications, and for evil consecrations.

In Jesus' name, I repent for generational divination, using tarot cards, psychic readings, palm readings, and Ouija boards.

I repent for all generational hexes, spells, and curses.

Lord, I repent on behalf of all my ancestors for using their Godly prophetic giftings for ungodly purposes.

I repent for all those who used their Godly gifts of signs, wonders, and healings for ungodly purposes.

In Jesus' name, I repent on behalf of all my ancestors for celebrating pagan festivals with homage to the gods, sacrifices, and self-dedications.

I repent on behalf of all my ancestors for mixing their faith in God with witchcraft, sorcery, and superstitious beliefs.

I repent for generational ancestral worship.

I repent for generational belief in fairies, leprechauns, gnomes, the Blarney Stone, and kissing the Blarney Stone.

Lord, I repent on behalf of all my ancestors for bathing in Stonehenge waters and believing in magical healings.

Lord, I repent for all generational use of black magic and for belief in omens.

Lord, I repent on behalf of all my ancestors for touching the dead for "good luck."

In Jesus' name, I repent for all cursing and blasphemy against God, the church, and the communion sacraments.

I repent for all generational blasphemy against the name of Jesus and blasphemy against the Holy Spirit.

I repent for all generational cursing of life and for all self-cursing.

In Jesus' name, I repent where I have sinned in these areas, and I ask that You would forgive me and release me from the consequences of these sins.

Please release me from the consequences of my ancestors' sins and stop the unfavorable reaping and sowing in my life.

I thank You, Jesus, that You are faithful and just to forgive us for all our sins and cleanse us of all unrighteousness.

In the name of Jesus, by the authority that Jesus gave me through the Cross, I close all demonic and occult doors that my ancestors opened.

Holy Spirit, please seal these doors shut that they are never to be opened again.

Holy Spirit, please open all Godly doors that were previously closed to me because of my ancestors' sins.

Thank you, Lord Jesus.

Amen.

Generational Prayer for Financial Release

In Jesus' name, I repent and renounce on behalf of all my ancestors from the beginning of time to the present for the stealing of land and the stealing of homes.

I repent and renounce for generational stealing of livelihoods, stealing of crops, and stealing of animals.

Lord, I repent on behalf of all my ancestors for the stealing of other people's inheritances, and for the stealing of family inheritances.

Lord, I repent on behalf of all my ancestors for betrayal, treason, greed, and hoarding of wealth. I repent for all generational deception, lies, slander, jealousy, and false accusations.

In Jesus' name, I repent on behalf of all my ancestors from the beginning of time to the present for sexual intimacy with prostitutes.

Lord, I repent on behalf of all my ancestors who were prostitutes and sold themselves for money. I repent for all generational infidelity, unfaithfulness, and promiscuity.

I repent for all generational earning or taking of blood money and for dishonest gain.

Lord, I repent on behalf of all my ancestors for all criminal activities.

I repent for all bribery and taking of bribes and for all dishonest scales, dishonest weights, and dishonest measures.

I repent for all generational hoarding and the withholding of funds for selfish purposes.

In Jesus' name, I repent on behalf of all my ancestors for ignoring the poor and for not taking care of widows and orphans.

I repent on behalf of all my ancestors for trusting in money instead of placing their trust in the Lord Jesus Christ. I repent for the idolatry of money.

Lord, I repent for all generational laziness and for burying talents.

I repent on behalf of all my ancestors for living a prosperous life using stolen money, stolen land, and stolen treasures.

Lord, I repent for their mockery of righteousness, Godliness, and integrity.

I repent for their drunkenness, gambling, and cheating.

I repent on behalf of all my ancestors for robbing people of their birthrights and causing their dreams, visions, and aspirations to be aborted.

I repent on behalf of all my ancestors for wrongful imprisonment and for perverting justice and the innocent.

I repent on behalf of all my ancestors for cheating on their income taxes and for exploiting the welfare system or the social system.

Lord, I repent on behalf of myself and all my ancestors for not rendering unto Caesar what rightfully belongs to him.

In Jesus' name, I repent for all generational ungodly vows of poverty, and for rejecting God's blessings.

Isaiah 5:18 - The Message (in my words):

In Jesus' name, I repent on behalf of all my ancestors from the beginning of time to the present who used lies to sell evil, who hauled sin to market by the truckload.

I repent on behalf of all by ancestors from the beginning of time to the present who challenged God and said, "What is God waiting for? Let Him move so we can see it."

61

I repent on behalf of all my ancestors who called evil good and good evil, who put darkness in place of light and light in place of darkness, who substituted bitter for sweet and sweet for bitter.

I repent for generational pride, arrogance, and self-sufficiency.

I repent on behalf of all my ancestors for being champion boozers, who collected trophies from drinking bouts.

I repent on behalf of all my ancestors for taking bribes from the guilty while violating the rights of the innocent.

I repent on behalf of all my ancestors from the beginning of time to the present who said "no" to the revelation of the God of Hosts and would have nothing to do with the God of Israel.

Lord Jesus, You died on the cross to pay the debt I could not pay.

I ask, Lord Jesus, that You would cover with Your blood that You shed on Calvary for my sins, to pay all the outstanding financial debts that are owing by my ancestors from the beginning of time to the present. These debts were incurred because of their lawlessness, greed, thievery, and sinful lifestyles.

Lord Jesus, please pay the outstanding debts of stolen inheritances, human suffering, lost birthrights, and lost visions and dreams that my ancestors owe, from the beginning of time to the present.

Thank You, Lord Jesus, that I am now debt free because of the finished work of the Cross. Amen.

9

Further Resources

If you are interested in learning more about generational curses, I recommend:

1. *Healing through Deliverance: The Foundation and Practice of Deliverance Ministry* by Peter Horrobin
2. *Transforming the Inner Man: God's Powerful Principles for Inner Healing and Lasting Life Change (Transformation)* by John Sandford

CPSIA information can be obtained
sting.com
JSA
31119
1B/1/P